THE WHOLE GOSPEL: REVISITING OUR MESSAGE TO THE WORLD

Q Society Room

A Group Learning Experience

Five Group Gatherings

NORTON HERBST AND GABE LYONS

ZONDERVAN.com/
AUTHORTRACKER
follow your favorite authors

ZONDERVAN

The Whole Gospel Participant's Guide
Copyright © 2010 Q

Requests for information should be addressed to:

Zondervan, *Grand Rapids, Michigan 49530*

ISBN 978-0-310-32519-2

All Scripture quotations, unless otherwise indicated, are taken from the Holy Bible, *Today's New International Version™. TNIV®.* Copyright © 2001, 2005 by Biblica, Inc.™ Used by permission of Zondervan. All rights reserved worldwide.

Any Internet addresses (websites, blogs, etc.) and telephone numbers printed in this book are offered as a resource. They are not intended in any way to be or imply an endorsement by Zondervan, nor does Zondervan vouch for the content of these sites and numbers for the life of this book.

All rights reserved. No part of this publication may be reproduced, stored in a retrieval system, or transmitted in any form or by any means—electronic, mechanical, photocopy, recording, or any other—except for brief quotations in printed reviews, without the prior permission of the publisher.

Published in association with Yates & Yates, www.yates2.com.

Printed in the United States of America

the whole gospel

TABLE OF CONTENTS

The Whole Gospel 1

Welcome to the Society Room 4

Your Place in Culture 6

Roundtable Discussions 8

Group Gathering One: Reframing the Gospel 11

Q Short: Spiritual Conversations 29

Group Gathering Two: Spiritual Conversations 45

Group Gathering Three: Cultural Commission 61

Group Gathering Four: To Write Love on Her Arms 79

Culture Shaping Project: Learning While Doing 96

Group Gathering Five: Whatever You Do for the Least 99

THE WHOLE GOSPEL: REVISITING OUR MESSAGE TO THE WORLD

The Bible is a story. Not like a children's fairytale or a sci-fi fantasy. But a grand story that tells us about God and his work in the world. So the Bible is also our story.

The way we share our story with others reveals the kind of gospel message we believe in. Unfortunately, many Christians have come to believe in a gospel that is only concerned with getting individuals to heaven. We think this is the chief message of the Bible. And then we go out and pitch this limited gospel to others in ways that devalue the holistic nature of the message itself. Could we have gotten it wrong?

In this Q Society Room experience, your group will be challenged to revisit the story of the Bible. You'll explore the richness of its themes and see how it shapes every aspect of our lives—what we believe, how we live, how we interact with culture, and how we share this "good news" with others.

THE WHOLE GOSPEL
WELCOME

WELCOME TO THE SOCIETY ROOM

Q Society Room studies are a new, yet historic way to consider issues of faith and culture in the context of a group learning environment. The Society Rooms of the late 1600s and the Clapham Circle of the early 1800s are riveting examples of small gatherings of leaders that would convene, dialogue, learn, and work together to renew their culture. Consider the impact of these early Society Rooms:

> In 1673 Dr. Anthony Horneck, a Church of England minister in London, preached a number of what he called "awakening sermons." As a result several young men began to meet together weekly in order to build up one another in the Christian faith. They gathered in small groups at certain fixed locations and their places of meeting became known as Society Rooms. In these gatherings they read the Bible, studied religious books and prayed; they also went out among the poor to relieve want at their own expense and to show kindness to all. By 1730 nearly one hundred of these Societies existed in London, and others—perhaps another hundred—were to be found in cities and towns throughout England. The Societies movement became, in many senses, the cradle of the Revival ..." (Arnold Dallimore, *George Whitefield*, Vol. 1, Crossway, 1990, pp. 28–29)

Following this historical example, this group study is designed to renew your minds as leaders so that you can make a difference in society. Society Room communities like yours are characterized by a commitment to put learning into action. And no doubt, over the course of the next few weeks, your innermost beliefs and preconceived ideas about life, faith, the world, and your cultural responsibility will be challenged. But that's the point.

Here's how it works. Your group will gather five times to discuss important topics related to the overall theme of this study. Sometimes you'll be given something to do or read before your group gathers. It's important for you to take these "assignments" seriously. They won't demand much time, but they will require intentionality. Doing these things ahead of time will cultivate a richer and more stimulating group experience as you begin to practice what you are learning.

For each group gathering, set aside about one hour and fifteen minutes for the discussion in a place with minimal distractions. Your group may want to share a meal together first, but be sure to allow enough time for unhurried dialogue to take place. Sometimes you'll watch a short video. But conversation and dialogue will always be the priority. The leader of the group will not teach or lecture, but instead will ask questions, facilitate conversation, and seek input from everyone. Be prepared to ask good questions and share your own thoughts. Sometimes you'll even debate an issue by taking sides and thinking through all the complexities. The goal of each gathering is for your group to be stimulated by a particular idea and learn together as you discuss its impact on your faith, your lives, and culture in general. Your group may not arrive at a consensus regarding any given topic. That's okay. Be respectful of others, even when you disagree with them. We can learn something from everyone.

Before your fifth gathering, you will undertake a group project together. You may be tempted to skip this. Don't! Your group project might be the most important part of your experience. Genuine learning as a community takes place when you engage the ideas you are discussing and do something together as a group.

In the end, be committed to this group and the learning process that is about to ensue. Your willingness to prepare for group gatherings, keep an open mind, and demonstrate eagerness to learn together will pave the way for a great experience.

YOUR PLACE IN CULTURE

INTRODUCTIONS

At the beginning of your first gathering, spend about fifteen minutes introducing yourselves to one another and discussing your channel of cultural influence.

There are several different social institutions that touch every person in a given society. These areas of influence contain most of the industries and organizations that consistently shape our culture. They touch every aspect of our lives, and most of us find our vocational roles in one or more of these areas. They are the seven channels of cultural influence.

As you begin your Society Room experience, you'll notice that most, if not all, of these channels are represented in your group. Start your first gathering by sharing which particular channel of influence you participate in. Give the rest of the group a sense of how your channel contributes to shaping society in general. Then, throughout the rest of the group experience, reflect on how your learning will affect the channel to which you've been called.

7

Channels of Cultural Influence

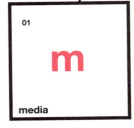

01

m

media

the whole gospel 7

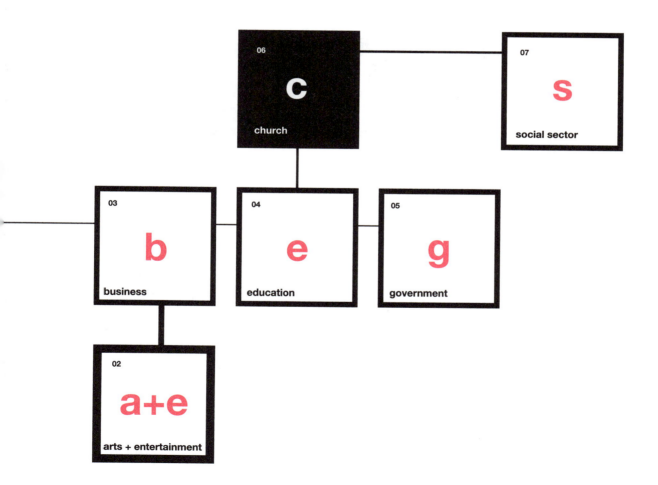

introduction

ROUNDTABLE DISCUSSIONS

As part of this Q Society Room, we convened leaders from various channels of culture to discuss these important topics. Throughout the study, you will be introduced to their thoughts and ideas in hopes of stirring your conversation and dialogue.

Gabe Lyons
Q Founder & Author
Gabe Lyons is the author of *The Next Christians: The Good News About the End of Christian America* and the creator of Q — a learning community that educates Christians on their responsibility and opportunities to renew culture. Lyons coauthored *UnChristian*, a bestselling book that reveals exclusive research on pop culture's negative perception of Christians. Gabe, his wife Rebekah, and their three children reside in Atlanta, Georgia.

Margaret Feinberg
Author & Speaker
Margaret was recently named by *Charisma* magazine as one of the "30 Emerging Voices" who will help lead the church in the next decade. She has written more than a dozen books, including the critically-acclaimed *The Organic God* and *The Sacred Echo*. People of all ages connect with her relational teaching style.

Tim Willard
Author
Tim Willard is a writer and content developer specializing in books, curriculum, and organizational messaging for such clients as Q, Catalyst, Orange, Chick-fil-A Leadercast, and Prison Entrepreneurship Program. He is currently finishing an MA in Christian Thought at Gordon-Conwell Theological Seminary. Tim is writing his first book *Veneer* due out in 2011 with Zondervan. He lives somewhere north of Atlanta with his wife, Chris, and two daughters, Lyric and Brielle.

Andy Crouch
Author & Journalist
Andy Crouch is the author of *Culture Making: Recovering Our Creative Calling* and a senior editor at Christianity Today International. He has served as executive producer of the documentary films *Where Faith and Culture Meet* and *Round Trip* and was editorial director of the Christian Vision Project. He is currently a member of the editorial board of *Books & Culture* and a senior fellow of the International Justice Mission's IJM Institute.

Jon Tyson
Pastor, New York City
Jon Tyson is a church planter and lead pastor of Trinity Grace Church, located in New York City. He is also on the board of directors of the Origins Movement, a new church planting movement committed to multiplying missional church communities in the major urban centers of the world.

We are lonesome animals. We spend all our life trying to be less lonesome. One of our ancient methods is to tell a story begging the listener to say—and to feel—Yes, that's the way it is, or at least that's the way I feel it. You're not as alone as you thought.

JOHN STEINBECK

The answer to the question "Who am I?" can only be given if we ask "What is my story?" and that can only be answered if there is an answer to the further question, "What is the whole story of which my story is a part?"

LESSLIE NEWBIGIN

God reveals himself to us not in a metaphysical formulation or a cosmic fireworks display but in the kind of stories that we use to tell our children who they are and how to grow up as human beings.

EUGENE PETERSON

GROUP GATHERING ONE
REFRAMING THE GOSPEL

group gathering one

YOUR STORY

DISCUSS

Take a few minutes and share "your story" with the rest of the group.

Our lives are like stories. They are made up of characters, conflicts, and above all, a meandering plotline full of triumphs and failures. Some people and events add richness to our narratives; others simply fill in the details. Still others challenge the very meaning of our stories. For people of faith, God's work in our lives is an underlying foundation to our stories. And our initial awareness of God's grace through his Son Jesus can often be a pivotal point or defining season in our lives.

DISCUSSION STARTERS

How did you first come to understand God's grace in your life?

Was it a pivotal moment or was it more of a slow awakening?

Are you still searching for spiritual answers and, if so, how have you sensed divine guidance in your life?

KEY COMPONENTS OF STORY

SETTING	the beginning of the story where characters and setting are established
CONFLICT	the problem(s) faced by the characters
RISING ACTION	events in the story leading up to the climax
CLIMAX	the culmination of events in the story where the conflict is engaged
FALLING ACTION	events leading to the solving of the story's problems
RESOLUTION	how events and problems of the story are solved

group gathering one

THE GOSPEL REVISTED

WATCH

View Q Talk: The Gospel Revisted by Tim Keel.

Record your thoughts on the talk on page 17.

Tim Keel is a lecturer and interim dean in the School of Mission and Ministry at Laidlaw College in Auckland, New Zealand. Before that, Tim served as the founding pastor of Jacob's Well in Kansas City, Missouri. He is also the author of *Intuitive Leadership: Embracing a Paradigm of Metaphor, Narrative, and Chaos*.

At Q Austin, Tim presented a talk on the nature of the gospel message. He challenged participants to return to the Bible and, specifically, to the Old Testament that shaped Jesus' worldview. It's there that we get a better picture of the story, or more accurately, the stories that Jesus used to frame God's gospel message.

the whole gospel 15

"I think we have a message problem. We have domesticated the gospel."

"I'm afraid we have a greater commitment to the categories, systems, and understandings of the gospel than the Person it is meant to reflect."

"The church has been obsessed with the priestly story. We've framed the gospel and Jesus almost exclusively through the priestly lens."

"Salvation is not just fall and redemption. It's creation, fall, redemption, restoration."

"What if the question went from: 'If you were to die tonight, where would you go?' to: 'If you knew you had twenty years, what kind of life would you want to live?' Jesus has a compelling answer to that question: 'Wake up, come and follow me.' "

the whole gospel 17

THOUGHTS

group gathering one

THE FOCUS OF OUR MESSAGE

DEBATE

Split the group into two sides* and spend fifteen minutes debating the issue:

Do you agree that we neglect the stories that Jesus engaged the most and ignore essential aspects of the gospel message?

Record your thoughts on each position on pages 20-21.

Use the following debate starters to guide your time.

Tim Keel asserts that Christians have focused too much on the priestly story—you are sinful and unclean and Jesus came to die for your sins and make you clean. Consequently, we neglect the stories that Jesus engaged the most—creation, exile, and exodus—and we ignore essential aspects of the gospel message. Do you agree?

DEBATE STARTERS

What compelling arguments did Tim Keel present?

Does it devalue the priestly story to also emphasize the other stories?

What are people's greatest needs: to be cleansed from their sins and made righteous (the priestly story), or to know their purpose in life, be liberated from addictions, and be restored from brokenness (the creation, exodus, and exile stories)?

Does the gospel message need to be reduced to one simple statement, or can it be a complex collection of stories that engage different kinds of people in different circumstances in different ways?

*Even if you don't agree with the side you are representing, consider and offer the best arguments for your position. Be respectful.

group gathering one

YES

The gospel message is much bigger than we often communicate.

THOUGHTS

NO

It's imperative to keep Jesus' death for our sins and the transaction that takes place when we trust him as the only focus and benefit of the gospel message.

THOUGHTS

group gathering one

THE KINGDOM OF GOD

REFLECT

Have a few people in your group take turns reading this section aloud.

Then journal your thoughts on pages 24-25.

When Jesus began teaching in Israel, he announced that there was "good news" for everyone. The Greek word that we translate as "gospel" in English (*euangelion*) literally means "good news." It was the same term used by the Romans to herald the crowning of a new emperor. It meant times were changing—a new ruler has taken the throne. So, what was the good news that Christ came to share?

The good news according to Jesus was that the kingdom of God had begun breaking into our world through Jesus himself. Listen to how Mark describes it.

> After John was put in prison, Jesus went into Galilee, proclaiming the good news (*euangelion*) of God. "The time has come," he said. "The kingdom of God has come near. Repent and believe the good news (*euangelion*)!"

– Mark 1:14–15

Consider what Jesus didn't say about this gospel. He didn't instill his listeners with fear of judgment. Rather, it was good news he was declaring. Nor did he say that there was now a way to go to heaven when you died (though he would talk about heaven at other times). Instead, he focused on something much greater that was happening now, in this world, in culture at large: the coming kingdom of God. Of course, this kingdom had future dimensions (eternal life), and without a doubt it compelled repentance and belief. But at its core, Jesus' message was that the kingdom of God had arrived, in some way, in the present. As New Testament scholar Craig Blomberg puts it, "Jesus' ministry is inaugurating a new era in human history" (*Jesus and the Gospels*, Broadman & Holman Academic, 2nd ed., 2009, p. 223).

REFLECTION STARTERS
Spend a few minutes journaling your thoughts to the three questions below. Then, share your reflections with the group.

The kingdom of God is the dominant theme in all of Jesus' teaching. Do you find that this concept is difficult to understand or explain? Why or why not?

It seems that the church has largely neglected this theme of the kingdom of God until recently. Would you agree? If so, why do you think that is the case?

How would it change your perspective on "sharing the gospel" with others if you focused more on God's powerful rule in this world and its implications for our lives?

24 group gathering one

the whole gospel

JOURNAL

THE GOOD NEWS

CONCLUDE

When Jesus died on a cross for our sins, he offered to forgive us and make us clean. But there is much more to the "good news" than this. We are recreated for the purposes for which God made us, liberated from the things that enslave us, and restored to the wholeness that only God can give us. This is indeed good news!

Which aspect of the gospel message do you think has the most significance in your channel of influence?

SPIRITUAL CONVERSATIONS

PREPARE FOR NEXT GATHERING

Before your next gathering, read the Q Short by Ron Martoia beginning on page 30. Be sure to set aside some uninterrupted time for this. Try not to save it until the last minute. When you read the essay, underline, highlight, or jot down comments about ideas that are particularly interesting, disconcerting, or challenging. Be prepared to share why at the next gathering.

Q SHORT

SPIRITUAL CONVERSATIONS: UNDERSTANDING THE CULTURAL LANGUAGE

SPIRITUAL CONVERSATIONS: UNDERSTANDING THE CULTURAL LANGUAGE

By Ron Martoia

I rarely see afternoon TV, but a few years ago I stumbled upon a twenty-minute segment and, wow, was it compelling. Through sobbing and tears, person after person began recounting how after watching a TV show one month earlier their lives had instantly and forever changed. "Instantly" and "forever" definitely caught my attention. They went on to talk about how they were now in charge of their lives, bringing to themselves any outcomes they chose. The teachers of the phenomenon made it clear it was all because "you create your own reality, and that as a spiritual being you bring your spirit to bear on the circumstances of life." I paused long enough to take in the details because of the confessed monumental change it brought. This was my introduction to *The Secret*, the most recent craze to hit American culture and propelled to cult status by current spiritual and philanthropy diva, Oprah.

Finding spiritual conversations in American culture is not hard. *The Secret* held the number one spot on the *New York Times* bestseller list for several months. PBS consistently airs Wayne Dyer, also a bestselling author, talking about his brand of spirituality. Tom Cruise and John Travolta unashamedly speak of their belief in Scientology. Madonna and a host of other celebrities espouse Kabbalah. While conversations about spiritual things seem acceptable and even in vogue, conversations about the Christian God are a different story. People don't seem to be nearly as open to that. Why the distinction? Yes to spiritual conversation, no to Christian conversation. Why is spirituality a raging interest in America, but the Christian version so marginalized?

I want to suggest that the Christian church, particularly the evangelical Christian version, is in a rut when it comes to having spiritual conversations. Part of the problem is our starting point. The way we start conversations about spirituality and the ensuing perspective we communicate cuts us out of a good deal of productive dialogue. And that means we have a message problem.

We essentially have a message that says you are screwed up and you need to be fixed. This is what we have classically referred to as the Fall-Redemption story. We are all sinners and God, who is holy, comes in and rescues us from the mess we have made. This conversation immediately leads us to talking about ourselves, and more importantly, talking about God, in ways that just aren't helpful. Our conversations aren't connecting with our current culture. Why is that? It might be because they aren't even connecting with us.

Let me ask you a question. I want you to answer based on how you reflexively feel, not on cognitive thought. When I say "God," do you reflexively *feel* a God who will help you soar, buoy you up, love you, and have your best interests in mind? Or do you instantly and reflexively *feel* a God who is "keeping track," watching how you will do, monitoring your basic performance?

If you are like most Christians who have participated in my ad hoc surveys over the last year or so, your instant reaction is probably the latter image of God as Judge, not the former image of God as Love. In settings where I have done this exercise, the vast majority of the people said God as Judge was their "no-thought-reflexive" response. What is interesting is that these business people, artists, musicians, ministers, and full-time stay-at-home parents acknowledge that this is not the image of God they actually try to teach or model to others. Nor is it what they publicly affirm or give verbal assent to. But it is reflexively what they feel. So we have a collision of what is deeply and reflexively believed and what is verbally stated as the "right answer," so to speak.

Foundationally, this reveals that Christians need to reexamine the nature of the gospel message and what it says about who God really is. It also has implications for our culture. If God is perceived as a judge by those of us *inside the club*, then what would you guess those outside of the church assume about him? Is it surprising that we are perceived as representing a judgmental, negative, nonaccepting, non-loving God? Is it any wonder people outside the church have negative views about the version of God propagated by those inside the church? No wonder the challenge seems so formidable.

So here is the summary of the problem: God is viewed as "out there," as "Other," as judgmental and ready to crack us into shape when we get out of line. God as a transcendent "Other" is clearly part of Christian belief; this should not be challenged. But if it is *part* of the Christian understanding, is it possible it is only a *part*? Is it possible there is more? Are we missing important aspects of how we can and should relate to God? And if so, is it possible that when we talk to others in our culture about God, there is a better starting point?

> GOD OUT THERE, GOD AS OTHER, IS GOD PERCEIVED AS JUDGMENTAL AND READY TO CRACK YOU WHEN YOU GET OUT OF LINE. BUT THE GOD OUT THERE, GOD AS SECOND PERSON IS THE ONLY CONVERSATION THE CHURCH KNOWS HOW TO HAVE.

THE REST OF THE STORY

The Fall-Redemption story is part of the story, but it is really an abbreviated lo-cal excerpt of the fuller version. And here is the problem: to start the conversation with the fall is to start talking about God's story at Genesis 3. Starting the conversation here and omitting the opening salvos of the first two chapters has locked us into having only one conversation about God—what I call the second person conversation. I would like to suggest that when we start the conversation with a Fall-Redemption paradigm, we can only talk about God in second person: as "Other" and "out there." While that is totally true about God, our inability to see God from other perspectives may be debilitating us.

Part of the way through this impasse is to start at the beginning of the story instead of Genesis 3. When we start the story in the creation narratives, the truncated Fall-Redemption story expands to the Creation-Fall-Redemption story. Humans are no longer viewed as fundamentally sinful and God no longer as only a judge. And this leads to a fourth concluding part of the story, which clarifies the reason for redemption and that is for the express purpose of getting us back to Eden, the creation. This fourth part we might call re-creation or restoration. This leads to a more holistic four-part story: Creation-Fall-Redemption-Restoration. And that changes how we begin to view God himself.

In Genesis 1 and 2, we actually have grounds for God conversations that start in a different place. In Genesis 1, we have God creating humanity *imago dei* (in the image of God). Here is a picture of God breathing into humanity his Spirit. What shape might a conversation take that has the *imago dei*, which is present in every human, as the starting place? In other words, what would a conversation look like that said "you have god-stuff in you"? In contrast to the second person view of God (as "Other," "out there," and Judge), this is what we might call the first person view of God. Part of him is actually in each of us. Culture seems to be having this kind of conversation all around us, but not *with* us.

Further, as God breathed into humanity, God's charge to humanity was to selflessly serve and oversee the created order. That included the animals they named, the flora they cultivated, the birds they sang with, and the fish that introduced them to the aquatic world below. Creation itself may provide yet another conversation entry point. Every time we see God in the sunset, acknowledge God in nature, and recognize God's presence in the complexity and wonder of the oceanic ecosystem, we are seeing God "out there," not as second person Judge, but as third person creation personified, so to speak.

I believe that we have to start having more first and third person conversations about God. These kinds of conversations are just as universal as the second person fall conversation, but they hold two huge advantages. First, they are positive starting points. Is it any wonder people don't gravitate toward the "you are heading to hell in a handbasket" conversation but do resonate with a "you have been made as the crowning glory of creation" conversation? Second, they are more biblical. First and third person conversations about God embrace the whole story of the gospel, not simply the half-story of Fall-Redemption.

For some of us, what I'm suggesting may be a foray into unknown waters. God in us? God in creation? Let me be clear. I'm not suggesting that we forsake the view that God is transcendent and wholly "Other." Nor am I suggesting that humanity being made in the image of God implies humans have the same powers or attributes of the Father, Son, and Holy Spirit. Nor am I suggesting that God is equal to creation in some kind of New Age, pantheistic fashion. But I do believe that seeing God in these first and third person ways is biblical. Indeed our brothers and sisters from the Eastern Orthodox tradition of Christianity may be able to substantially help us along here. And I suggest that if we stick only to our second person conversation about God, we might be missing a valuable and universal starting point to introduce people to the kind of life-changing message of the gospel they are so desperately seeking.

GOD IN US

In our Protestant church tradition we don't have many categories for understanding this first person, God-within pursuit. But Scripture teaches this first person perspective. Consider these passages in light of this first person conversation (all references TNIV, emphasis added).

His divine power has given us everything we need for a godly life through our knowledge of him who called us by his own glory and goodness. Through these he has given us his very great and precious promises, so that through them *you may participate in the divine nature*, having escaped the corruption in the world caused by evil desires (2 Peter 1:3–4).

Dear friends, now we are children of God, and what we will be has not yet been made known. But we know that when Christ appears, we shall be like him, for *we shall see him* as he is (1 John 3:2).

To them God has chosen to make known among the Gentiles the glorious riches of this mystery, which is *Christ in you*, the hope of glory (Col. 1:27).

Don't you know that you yourselves are *God's temple* and that God's Spirit dwells in your midst? If anyone destroys God's temple, God will destroy that person; for God's temple is sacred, and you together are that temple (1 Cor. 3:16–17).

Do you not know that your bodies are *temples of the Holy Spirit*, who is in you, whom you have received from God? You are not your own (1 Cor. 6:19).

ARE WE LETTING OUR CURRENT
CULTURAL CONDITIONS AND FEAR
INFLUENCE HOW WE READ PASSAGES
OF SCRIPTURE THAT THOSE IN OTHER
TIME PERIODS SEEMED TO
SEE SO CLEARLY?

"We are not stoning you for any good work," they replied, "but for blasphemy, because you, a mere man, claim to be God." Jesus answered them, "Is it not written in your Law, 'I have said you are "gods" '? If he called them 'gods,' to whom the word of God came—and Scripture cannot be broken—what about the one whom the Father set apart as his very own and sent into the world? Why then do you accuse me of blasphemy because I said, 'I am God's Son'? (John 10:33–36)

Of course, there is no way for us to do full commentary on these passages. But we do need to note these passages make it sound as if a journey inward toward God, first person, is just as legitimate as a journey outward toward God, second person.

Let's briefly look at the John 10 passage. And what is most disquieting about Jesus' words isn't just that the word *god* was used of humans, but that those being spoken to in the passage are the Pharisees, not Christ-following, "filled with the Spirit" disciples. While the other passages are presumably aimed at Christians, this passage isn't. Consider what one theologian and defender of the Christian faith has said about this passage.

Morality is indispensable: but the Divine Life, which gives itself to us and which calls us to be gods, intends for us something in which morality will be swallowed up. We are to be remade. . . . We shall find underneath it all a thing we have never yet imagined: a real man, an ageless god, a son of God, strong, radiant, wise, beautiful, and drenched in joy.[1]

(God) said that we were "*gods*" and He is going to make good His words. If we let Him—for we can prevent Him if we choose—He will make the feeblest and filthiest of us into a god or goddess, dazzling, radiant, immortal creature, pulsating all through with such energy and joy and wisdom and love as we cannot now imagine, a bright stainless mirror which reflects back to God perfectly (though, of course, on a smaller scale) His own boundless power and delight and goodness. The process will be long and in parts very painful; but that is what we are in for.[2]

Shocked at C. S. Lewis? Many people are quite shocked to realize he had a very developed first person perspective. In the Protestant tradition we have a variety of words or terms we would use to describe the idea Lewis is getting at. We would call this becoming more like Christ, or using the Pauline term of "being conformed to the image of his Son," or "more of him, less of me." The idea of "union with Christ" is in focus. In a wide variety of our Christian traditions, including the theology of John Calvin and the Wesley brothers, one of two words often crops up in describing this idea of union: *theosis* or *divinization*. These are rich theological concepts. But I quote Lewis here to help us see that this first person understanding of God isn't relegated to some ascetic monks in an Eastern Orthodox monastery in Siberia. This is a topic that finds lots of outlet and expression in much of our Christian history, both ancient and modern.

I think we are reticent to engage a concept like this and maybe even fearful, because it is risky language. But when we recognize that God wants us to be little gods, then we begin to know God in new and fresh ways. In other words, a question arises: are we letting our current cultural conditions and fear influence how we read passages of Scripture that those in other time periods seemed to see so clearly?

I think the best way to safeguard ourselves from the charge of this being too New Age-y is to recognize that while we are called to be gods, our god-ness *is always derivative and therefore diminutive*. This is a critical distinction that prevents putting humanity on the same level as the Triune God, but at the same time acknowledges and engages what appears to be the full intent of the biblical material. Whatever it means that we are made in the image of God and have the breath of God within us, it certainly does not mean we are in every way shape and form identical to the Triune God, the Creator of the Universe. There is a distinction between Creator and the created. There is a qualitative and unique difference between the Maker and the made. As the created and made ones, whatever similarities and likenesses we have *are derived from the God who made us*. As a result of being derived, we are less than the Creator. This is the safeguard and clarification of how we can have the first person conversation while allowing the Triune God to remain God as "Other." And yet at the same time we can be *imago dei*, little gods, as Jesus says.

Lots of issues could be raised here and lots of material commented on and debated, but here is my hope. Is it possible the *imago dei*, as the common thread of all human beings, is the best starting point for spiritual conversations because it is something intuitively present? All of the current cultural conversations on spirituality have deep first person god tonality and it seems most people instantly gravitate toward and understand them. Most people "get" they are somehow god, or have God within, or have a seed of the divine.

Of course, many first person understandings people have about being god or having God within them are uninformed by the Bible and often inaccurate. But we are crazy not to wonder what theological basis there might be for this universal sense. And while we may not think people have this first person god thing right, most Christians don't have it right either: we only see God as Judge, not as Love, and rarely *in us*. Consequently, I think we need to radically reconsider all possible arenas of inquiry into how we think a journey toward God must proceed. These sorts of "reading the Bible again with a different perspective" exercises require significant humility and a willingness to realize we may not have it all figured out.

GOD IN CREATION

So let's review. We in the church are more than willing to have the second person, God as Other conversation with people. Our culture isn't so interested in that and is quite convinced the church is a pretty judgmental and negative place. So while many remain spiritually interested, the church probably won't be the primary laboratory for their exploration. Furthermore, culture is having all sorts of conversations about the god within, a sort of first person understanding of God. Those conversations are happening on the national bestseller list, daytime TV, and chat boards across the Internet. But the church? Well, we are uncomfortable with *that* conversation because it is New Age mumbo jumbo and it isn't the second person, God as Other conversation, which is the only one we are familiar with.

There is yet another conversation the culture is having that I mentioned earlier: the third person conversation about God. God as "out there," but not as a Judge, but as found and experienced in creation. Alongside the books and conversations about these first person god topics, there is a huge contingent of people that are increasingly concerned about the environment and Mother Earth and the living, breathing organism of creation. This is the third person "It" view of God, if you will. Whatever you think about the environment is secondary. Adam's quite literal physical connection to the dirt (*adamah* in Hebrew, with Adam's name being *adam*) and he and Eve being given a mandate to take care of the earth should be enough for us to recognize people are hovering over material we should be willing to have God conversations about. Certainly one of the more hopeful conversations going on in the church today is the need for us to be tuned into the creation, the environment, God's earth he's given us to steward.

Again, before you take caution, let's return to the Bible. There are many passages that seem to indicate an intimate connection between God and creation. Consider Psalm 19 (TNIV):

> The heavens declare the glory of God;
>   the skies proclaim the work of his hands.

> Day after day they pour forth speech;
> > night after night they display knowledge.
> They have no speech, they use no words;
> > no sound is heard from them.
> Yet their voice goes out into all the earth,
> > their words to the ends of the world.
> In the heavens he has pitched a tent for the sun,
> > which is like a bridegroom coming out of his chamber,
> > > like a champion rejoicing to run his course.
> It rises at one end of the heavens
> > and makes its circuit to the other;
> > > nothing is deprived of its warmth.
> – Psalm 19:1–6

Creation here is intimately linked to God. In a passage like this, creation is personified as speaking, as God actually telling us something about himself. Romans 8 (TNIV) seems to be the New Testament counterpart to a passage like Psalm 19.

> I consider that our present sufferings are not worth comparing with the glory that will be revealed in us. The creation waits in eager expectation for the children of God to be revealed. For the creation was subjected to frustration, not by its own choice, but by the will of the one who subjected it, in hope that the creation itself will be liberated from its bondage to decay and brought into the freedom and glory of the children of God. We know that the whole creation has been groaning as in the pains of childbirth right up to the present time (Romans 8:18–22).

Again, creation is personified as living, breathing, longing, and injured.

Of course, other passages could be listed, but the point is clear: God has a deep connection with creation. And note that we didn't say God *is* creation. Just like the first person God caveats we noted, we need to offer third person God caveats as well. We need to maintain a view of God that says God is distinct from creation but intimately invested in and working in and through creation. And the issue is getting momentum these days. If Oprah is the goddess of the first person god conversation, people like Thomas Berry and Al Gore are the apostles of the third person god conversation.

Until recently, the Christian conversation about ecology and God's creation was mostly relegated to those who were considered tree-hugging liberals. But not so anymore. This is an issue that more and more people in the church are starting to realize is part and parcel of the very story we have been invited to live, a story that starts in the garden of Eden. And even though cultural conversations often go too far in deifying creation, we have within our Christian tradition and theological repertoire adequate and legitimate resources to enter into powerful conversations about God in creation.

READING THE SIGNS

I can talk to any of my investigating friends about being made like God or having a charge from God to take care of creation, and every one of them instantly gets that and understands what I am talking about. When I use that entry point into the conversation, I am starting where they are, not where I wish them to be. When I start there, I open the possibilities of entering into second person conversations about God as Other, about the God who made creation, about the God that put this intuitive sense in them that they are divine or somehow connected to the divine. But this is not the whole story; it's just part of the story. We are not just fallen creatures in need of redemption. We are *created* in God's image, *corrupted* by sin, *redeemed* by his atoning work, and *restored* to pursue a life of wholeness, meaning, mission, and connection with God in holistic first, second, and third person ways.

I am afraid that as long as Christianity is primarily understood as a batch of propositions that position God as a Judge of how well you execute them, we have missed the larger story. And we will have problems getting other people interested in the story. Perhaps their lack of interest may be a good thing. Their rejection of our truncated, abbreviated Fall-Redemption story may be the very thing we need to get us to read the story again to see if we have it right.

What I have been suggesting here is an exercise in what is called semiotics. The Greek word *semion* in the Gospel accounts is the word for "sign." You may remember Jesus saying, "You know how to interpret the appearance of the sky, but you cannot interpret the signs of the times" (Matt. 16:3b). Semiotics is reading the signs of the times.

As we read culture, we see a couple of signs that give us hints and clues to entry points into conversations we just haven't understood how to have. My experience is that while there might be initial resistance by Christians to think in these ways, they are simply looking for "biblical permission" to interact around these topics because they are so common in the cultural airspace.

Semiotics is exactly what Jesus and the early Christians used as they interacted with others outside the faith. They met people where they were, expanded on their current understandings, and then challenged them to consider the movement of God in their lives. This wasn't a compromise. It was a commitment to God's grand story, to what he had already written on the hearts of seekers, to spiritual conversation engagements that met people at the intersection points of their interests and journeys.

Dr. Ron Martoia *is a transformational architect. Ron helps people and the organisms they serve design and then journey through the experience of deep change. Ron's doctorate is in the area of leadership and culture. In addition to having served on adjunct faculty at several universities, Ron has provided leadership training and organizational development in twelve countries around the world.*

END NOTES

[1] C. S. Lewis, *The Grand Miracle* (New York: Ballantine, 1986), 85.

[2] C. S. Lewis, *Mere Christianity* (New York: Collier, 1952), 174-5.

42 q short

THOUGHTS

the whole gospel 43

THOUGHTS

Ideal conversation must be an exchange of thought, and not, as many of those who worry most about their shortcomings believe, an eloquent exhibition of wit or oratory.

EMILY POST

The true spirit of conversation consists in building on another man's observation, not overturning it.

EDWARD G. BULWER-LYTTON

There is no such thing as a worthless conversation, provided you know what to listen for. And questions are the breath of life for a conversation.

JAMES NATHAN MILLER

GROUP GATHERING TWO
SPIRITUAL CONVERSATIONS

YOUR VIEW OF GOD

DISCUSS

In his essay, Ron Martoia suggested an exercise: "Let me ask you a question. I want you to answer based on how you reflexively feel, not on cognitive thought. When I say 'God,' do you reflexively feel a God who will help you soar, buoy you up, love you, and have your best interests in mind? Or do you instantly and reflexively feel a God who is 'keeping track,' watching how you will do, monitoring your basic performance?"

DISCUSSION STARTERS

How do you answer this question?

What has shaped your view of God the most?

Is there dissonance between how you subconsciously view God and what you say you believe about him? Why?

BELIEF IN GOD IN THE U.S.

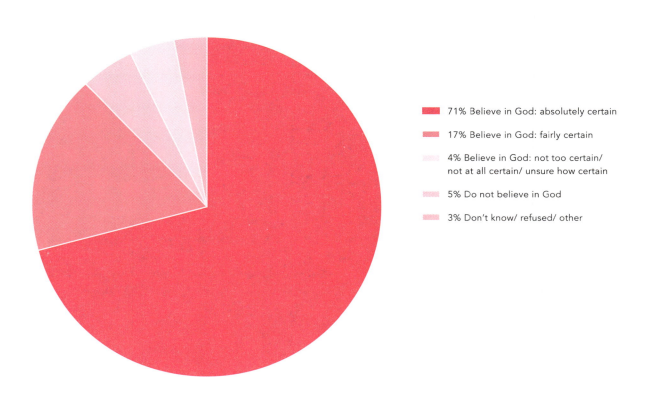

Source: The Pew Forum on Religion and Public Life: "U.S. Religious Landscape Survey," 2007 at http://religions.pewforum.org.

group gathering two

PERSPECTIVE OF GOD

DEBATE

Split the group into two sides* and spend twenty minutes debating the issue:

Do you think Ron Martoia's three ways of understanding God are helpful, or are compromises?

Record your thoughts on each position on pages 50-51.

Use the following debate starters to guide your time.

Ron Martoia differentiates between three ways of viewing God and the resulting conversations we have with others about him:

- First person perspective: God within us
- Second person perspective: God as an "out there" Judge
- Third person perspective: God as in creation

The first and third person perspectives seem more mystical, mysterious, and maybe unfamiliar to many of us.

Do you think these are helpful ways of understanding God, or compromises?

DEBATE STARTERS

What does it really mean for human beings to be made in God's image?

How does how we view God relate to our understanding of the gospel message?

What are the most difficult or threatening aspects of the first and third person perspectives of God?

What are the weaknesses of just sticking with the second person perspective of God?

Even if you don't agree with the side you are representing, consider and offer the best arguments for your position. Be respectful.

group gathering two

YES

The first and third person perspectives are biblical and we should incorporate them more into our thinking and conversations.

THOUGHTS

NO

I fear that these ways of understanding and talking about God compromise who he really is for the sake of being relevant.

THOUGHTS

AT THE AREOPAGUS

REFLECT

Have a few people in your group take turns reading this section aloud.

Then journal your thoughts on pages 55-57.

It's the first-century AD Roman Empire. Much like today, there are small bands of Christians trying to live out their faith among so many others who do not share their convictions. In fact, most of the great thinkers of the Roman Empire mock Christians for their seemingly absurd belief in one God who created the universe, and that this one God became a man named Jesus. Enter the apostle Paul.

During one of his travels throughout Greece, Paul stopped over in the cosmopolitan crossroads of Athens. It's here that he was confronted with the darkness and corruption of a first-century global city. Athens was known for its deeply religious, but extremely pluralistic environment: the city was filled with temples, shrines, statues, altars, and idols—all to the different gods that people worshiped. But Paul worshiped the one, true God, believing all the others were false. So how did he respond? How did he enter into conversation with these idol-worshiping "pagans"? Look at how history records his engagement:

> While Paul was waiting for [his friends] in Athens, he was greatly distressed to see that the city was full of idols. So he reasoned in the synagogue with both Jews and God-

fearing Greeks, as well as in the marketplace day by day with those who happened to be there. A group of Epicurean and Stoic philosophers began to debate with him. Some of them asked, "What is this babbler trying to say?" Others remarked, "He seems to be advocating foreign gods." They said this because Paul was preaching the good news about Jesus and the resurrection. Then they took him and brought him to a meeting of the Areopagus, where they said to him, "May we know what this new teaching is that you are presenting? You are bringing some strange ideas to our ears, and we would like to know what they mean." (All the Athenians and the foreigners who lived there spent their time doing nothing but talking about and listening to the latest ideas.)

Paul then stood up in the meeting of the Areopagus and said: "People of Athens! I see that in every way you are very religious. For as I walked around and looked carefully at your objects of worship, I even found an altar with this inscription: TO AN UNKNOWN GOD. So you are ignorant of the very thing you worship—and this is what I am going to proclaim to you.

"The God who made the world and everything in it is the Lord of heaven and earth and does not live in temples built by hands. And he is not served by human hands, as if he needed anything. Rather, he himself gives everyone life and breath and everything else. From one man he made all the nations, that they should inhabit the whole earth; and he marked out their appointed times in history and the boundaries of their lands. God did this so that they would seek him and perhaps reach out for him and find him, though he is not far from any one of us. 'For in him we live and move and have our being.' As some of your own poets have said, 'We are his offspring.'

"Therefore since we are God's offspring, we should not think that the divine being is like gold or silver or stone—an image made by human design and skill. In the past God overlooked such ignorance, but now he commands all people everywhere to repent. For he has set a day when he will judge the world with justice by the man he has appointed. He has given proof of this to everyone by raising him from the dead."

When they heard about the resurrection of the dead, some of them sneered, but others said, "We want to hear you again on this subject." At that, Paul left the Council. Some of the people became followers of Paul and believed. Among them was Dionysius, a member of the Areopagus, also a woman named Damaris, and a number of others.

– Acts 17:16–34

REFLECTION STARTERS

Spend a few minutes journaling your thoughts to the three questions below. Then, share your reflections with the group.

What do you think is significant about how Paul engages the philosophers and people of Athens at the Areopagus?

It's clear that Paul does not ignore his belief in God as a transcendent Judge (the second person perspective), but in what ways does he interact with their beliefs?

What can Christians learn from Paul about how we should interact with those who hold beliefs different than us?

56 group gathering two

JOURNAL

JOURNAL

group gathering two

A BIGGER GOD

CONCLUDE

The way we share our beliefs with others reveals what we believe in. And if we think that our message should be life-changing, yet it rarely engages others, we must rethink our message. God is indeed a Judge. But he's also made us in his image and revealed himself to all in creation. And this is good news.

How do friends within your circle of influence view God and how could you transform their perspective in the way you talk about God with them?

CULTURAL COMMISSION

PREPARE FOR NEXT GATHERING

Have a spiritual conversation with someone else—in a coffee shop, a pub, the gym, at school, the workplace, wherever you interact with others. Don't force it, and don't feel like you need to "share the gospel" the way we traditionally think about it. In fact, see the conversations that you already have with people as having a spiritual potential. Look for opportunities to talk about the spiritual journey all humans are on as we seek to better understand who we are and what purpose we were made for. Or discuss the beauty of creation and how transcendent or refreshing it can be for our souls. This, too, is sharing God's good news.

PREPARING FOR YOUR CULTURE SHAPING PROJECT

In the next few weeks, your group will take part in a project together to apply what you are learning and discussing. It's important that you complete this project before your last gathering. Three options for what your group can do have been recommended on pages 96–97. All of them require some planning and preparation. Take a few minutes now to read the options and discuss which one best suits your group. You don't have to make a decision this week, but you need to get the ball rolling and be prepared to make a decision and start planning at your next group meeting.

Worldviews are the basic stuff of human existence, the lens through which the world is seen, the blueprint for how one should live in it, and above all the sense of identity and place that enables human beings to be what they are. To ignore worldviews, either our own or those of the culture we are studying, would result in extraordinary shallowness.

N.T. WRIGHT

Creatures of a very particular making, we need to know the cultural blinders that narrow our worldview as well as the psychological blinders that narrow our view of our personal experience.

CHRISTINA BALDWIN

In the total expanse of human life there is not a single square inch of which the Christ, who alone is sovereign, does not declare, "That is mine!"

ABRAHAM KUYPER

GROUP GATHERING THREE
CULTURAL COMMISSION

group gathering three

YOUR WORLDVIEW

DISCUSS

Spend a few minutes sharing the two or three factors listed to the right that you believe have been most influential in shaping your worldview.

Everyone has a worldview. Chuck Colson and Nancy Pearcey define this as "the sum total of our beliefs about the world, the 'big picture' that directs our daily decisions and actions" (*How Now Shall We Live?*, Tyndale, 1999, p. 14).

WHAT HAS MOST MOST SHAPED YOUR WORLDVIEW AND WHY?

YOUR PARENTS OR FAMILY OF ORIGIN

WHERE YOU GREW UP

YOUR EDUCATION

YOUR POLITICAL VIEWS

YOUR FAITH TRADITION/DENOMINATION

YOUR PERSONALITY

YOUR SPOUSE AND/OR CHILDREN

DIFFICULT CIRCUMSTANCES IN LIFE

A PARTICULAR AUTHOR, MUSICIAN, OR FILMMAKER

THE BIBLE

YOUR HOBBIES

YOUR VOCATION

YOUR SOCIOECONOMIC SITUATION

A DEFINING EVENT

WHERE YOU CURRENTLY LIVE

group gathering three

CULTURAL COMMISSION

WATCH

View Q Talk: Cultural Commission by Charles Colson.

Record your thoughts on the talk on page 67.

Charles Colson is the founder of Prison Fellowship International, a ministry dedicated to criminal justice reform through faith-based programs. He is also a popular speaker and prolific author. His most recent book is entitled *The Faith: What Christians Believe, Why They Believe It, and Why It Matters*.

At Q New York, Charles Colson challenged listeners to reflect on their worldviews. He suggested that the Bible presents a holistic worldview that should shape what every Christian believes about reality. And most importantly, this Christian worldview does not simply address individuals and their eternal destinies, but also God's redemption of entire systems and cultures in the world.

the whole gospel 65

"All reality, all truth that can ever be known, is in the person of Jesus. He's the creator as well as the redeemer. Christianity is an explanation of all reality. . . . The implications of thinking about Christianity as a worldview are absolutely life-changing and transforming."

"Basically, we're ignorant. If we knew what we believed and if we really took it to heart, we would all be changing the world around us where we live and we'd be doing it in a winsome loving way."

"We've got a great message, all we need to do is understand it and see it as the kingdom. Don't reduce it down to something that's manageable to you, but live it out."

THOUGHTS

group gathering three

INDIVIDUALS VS. CULTURE

DEBATE

Split the group into two sides* and spend fifteen minutes debating the issue:

Should we focus on sharing our faith with individual people, or is transforming culture just as important?

Record your thoughts on each position on pages 70-71.

Use the following debate starters to guide your time.

Charles Colson asserts that one of the chief reasons Christians do not "live out" the gospel message is because we don't understand its holistic implications. Perhaps we believe that the gospel is only important for saving people's souls. Doing good works and making an impact on culture at large is good, but secondary. Do you agree? Should we focus on sharing our faith with individual people, or is transforming culture just as important?

DEBATE STARTERS

Doesn't the Great Commission (Matt. 28:19–20) demonstrate that our focus should be on evangelism and discipleship?

What was the purpose of the Law that God gave to Israel: to order their society around his principles or to demonstrate their sinfulness and need for a savior?

What are the disadvantages to only focusing on evangelism?

What are the disadvantages to only focusing on cultural transformation? Is it possible to give equal weight to both?

Even if you don't agree with the side you are representing, consider and offer the best arguments for your position. Be respectful.

group gathering three

YES

Our focus should be evangelism; everything else is secondary.

THOUGHTS

NO

Making a difference in culture at large (even if people don't become Christians) is equally important.

THOUGHTS

group gathering three

THE WHOLE CITY IN AN UPROAR

REFLECT

Have a few people in the group take turns reading this section aloud.

Then journal your thoughts on pages 74-75.

When Christians take their cultural commission seriously, it can produce powerful change for the common good of all in a society (as Colson's work in prisons demonstrates). On the other hand, the gospel is often countercultural. At times, it can even threaten, challenge, or overturn the governing systems and structures of our culture.

Paul and the early Christians had experiences like that on several occasions. Consider this instance when Christianity (also known as "the Way") was growing in Ephesus:

> About that time there arose a great disturbance about the Way. A silversmith named Demetrius, who made silver shrines of Artemis, brought in no little business for the skilled workers there. He called them together, along with the workers in related trades, and said: "You know, my friends, that we receive a good income from this business. And you see and hear how this fellow Paul has convinced and led astray large numbers of people here in Ephesus and in practically the whole province of Asia. He says that gods made by human hands are no gods at all. There is danger not only that our trade will lose its good name, but also that the temple of the

great goddess Artemis will be discredited; and the goddess herself, who is worshiped throughout the province of Asia and the world, will be robbed of her divine majesty."

When they heard this, they were furious and began shouting: "Great is Artemis of the Ephesians!" Soon the whole city was in an uproar. The people seized Gaius and Aristarchus, Paul's traveling companions from Macedonia, and all of them rushed together into the theater. Paul wanted to appear before the crowd, but the disciples would not let him. Even some of the officials of the province, friends of Paul, sent him a message begging him not to venture into the theater.
– Acts 19:23–31

Perhaps you've never started a riot. But in this case, the spread of the gospel wasn't just transforming lives; it was challenging the economic and financial livelihood of the whole city.

REFLECTION STARTERS
Spend a few minutes journaling your thoughts to the two questions below. Then, share your reflections with the group.

Have you seen an example in your city or culture where Christians met resistance when their efforts threatened the stability of culture?

What are some current practices, systems, or accepted norms in your city or cultural channel of influence that Christians should be challenging?

group gathering three

JOURNAL

JOURNAL

REDEEMING AND RESTORING ALL THINGS

CONCLUDE

God is not only concerned with individuals. Nor is he only interested in our "spiritual pursuits"—prayer, reading the Bible, going to church, etc. Everything is spiritual. The Christian worldview understands that God desires to bring redemption and restoration to all things—individuals, families, neighborhoods, cities, political systems, and entire cultures.

Which area—evangelism, discipleship, or cultural renewal—are you least engaged in as you consider your cultural channel of influence?

TO WRITE LOVE ON HER ARMS

PREPARE FOR NEXT GATHERING

Before your next gathering, set aside about thirty minutes to write down a definition of the gospel. First, write two or three paragraphs explaining what you believe the holistic nature of the gospel message is. Be comprehensive. Then second, try to summarize the gospel in one sentence. There is no "right answer." The Bible itself offers many different ways of explaining the gospel. But do your best to incorporate what you are learning in one succinct explanation of God's gospel message for our world.

Spend the final portion of your time together discussing your culture shaping project.

PLANNING THE CULTURE SHAPING PROJECT

You'll need to make a decision by the end of this gathering since what you do will likely require planning. Your project needs to take place before your last group gathering and it should be something that everyone can participate in. You can review the suggestions given on pages 96–97. It may be difficult to find total agreement among the group, but try to establish some consensus by talking through the advantages and disadvantages of all suggestions. Don't be afraid to think creatively and challenge yourselves. You're not limited by the suggestions included in this study, but you'll want to undertake something that will help you apply what you've been learning. Make a decision and solidify action steps before you conclude.

The gospel is more like a piece of music to be performed than a list of ideas to endorse.

SCOT MCKNIGHT

We can do no great things, only small things with great love.

MOTHER TERESA

God is love. Whoever lives in love lives in God, and God in them. This is how love is made complete among us so that we will have confidence on the day of judgment: In this world we are like Jesus.

1 JOHN 4:16B–17

GROUP GATHERING FOUR
TO WRITE LOVE ON HER ARMS

group gathering four

LOVE IS A VERB

DISCUSS

At the heart of the gospel message is love: God's love for us and us sharing that love with others. In America, the word *love* serves many functions: a little girl "loves" her dolls, a fan "loves" his football team, a wife "loves" her husband, a soldier "loves" his country.

DISCUSSION STARTERS

How would you define the kind of love God demonstrates toward us? How can we show that same love to others?

Jesus instructed his followers to love their enemies. Who are your enemies and how can you love them?

FOUR GREEK WORDS FOR LOVE

1. STORGE: AFFECTION, AS BETWEEN A PARENT AND CHILD

2. PHILIA: FRIENDSHIP, COMPANIONSHIP

3. EROS: PASSIONATE LOVE, REFERS TO SENSUAL DESIRE AND LONGING

4. AGAPE: SELF-SACRIFICING LOVE THAT ACTS IN THE BEST INTERESTS OF ANOTHER PERSON

"But God demonstrates his own love [agape] for us in this: While we were still sinners, Christ died for us."
– Romans 5:8

group gathering four

TO WRITE LOVE ON HER ARMS

WATCH

View Q Talk: To Write Love on Her Arms by Jamie Tworkowski.

Record your thoughts on the talk on page 85.

It began with a simple act of love. For five days, friends took care of Renee as she battled addiction, depression, self-injury, and attempted suicide before checking into rehab. Little did they know the impact their actions would have on all the other Renees of the world. As Jamie Tworkowski chronicled their story and word got out, a movement of love, hope, and redemption emerged. This is beauty. Listen as Jamie tells his amazing story.

the whole gospel 83

"We are only asked to love, to offer hope to the many hopeless. We don't get to choose all the endings, but we're asked to play the rescuers. We won't solve all the mysteries, and our hearts will certainly break in such a vulnerable life. But it is the best way. We were made to be lovers, in bold and broken places, pouring ourselves out again and again until we are called home."

"We had the opportunity to lead this conversation about things people don't talk much about, and that the church oftentimes doesn't talk about."

"We're trying to introduce people to the kingdom, without telling them in the first thirty seconds that it's the kingdom and they need to sign up for something."

THOUGHTS

THE CHURCH AS A LOVING COMMUNITY

DEBATE

Split the group into two sides* and spend fifteen minutes debating the issue:

Have churches dropped the ball when it comes to addressing the brokenness that exists in our culture?

Record your thoughts on each position on pages 88-89.

Use the following debate starters to guide your time.

There's no question that Jamie's response to Renee and the widespread problem of depression is admirable. Nevertheless, the church has often yielded dealing with such societal issues to professionals. Psychologist Larry Crabb suggests that this is a mistake. He asserts, "The crisis of care in modern culture, especially in the Western church, will not be resolved by training more therapists.… Beneath all our problems, there are desperately hurting souls that must find the nourishment only [Christian] community can provide" (*Connecting*, Word Publishing, 1997, p. xvi).

Is he right? Have churches dropped the ball when it comes to addressing the brokenness that exists in our culture?

DEBATE STARTERS

If the gospel message is rooted in God's love and restoration for all people, how do local churches live this out?

Is the root issue that people just don't have a personal relationship with God?

Are there some societal problems that local churches shouldn't address?

How can Christians and churches engage dark places in our world and stay true to their moral values?

Even if you don't agree with the side you are representing, consider and offer the best arguments for your position. Be respectful.

group gathering four

YES

The gospel best engages the world's problems through the healing environment of Christian community—the church.

THOUGHTS

NO

Churches are largely incapable of dealing with complex issues like depression, addictions, crime, family dysfunction, homelessness, and poverty.

THOUGHTS

BRINGERS OF THE MESSAGE OF SALVATION

REFLECT

Dietrich Bonhoeffer was a German theologian and pastor who resisted the rise of Nazism and was ultimately executed by Hitler near the end of World War II. In his book *Life Together*, he declares: "the goal of all Christian community: they meet one another as bringers of the message of salvation" (Harper & Row, 1954, p. 23).

REFLECTION STARTERS

Spend a few minutes journaling your thoughts to the three questions below. Then, share your reflections with the group.

When you gather with other Christians (informally as friends, in a small group, at church), how are you acting as a "bringer of the message of salvation" to one another?

How should Christian communities be "bringers of the message of salvation" to the wider world in both word and deed?

When we consider our role in the world, why do we often think in individual terms and rarely in communal terms?

group gathering four

JOURNAL

the whole gospel

JOURNAL

PEOPLE OF LOVE

`CONCLUDE`

We demonstrate our full understanding of the gospel when we love other people—especially those who seem unlovable. And we can't do this alone. It takes a loving community to truly embody God's love for our world.

In what ways have you loved those you encounter in your neighborhood, social circles, and workplace?

CULTURE SHAPING PROJECT

PREPARE FOR NEXT GATHERING

Your primary assignment is to undertake your culture shaping project before your next gathering. Be intentional about setting aside time to prepare for and execute your project so that you can discuss it when you next meet. Project options follow on pages 96–97.

CULTURE SHAPING PROJECT

IDEAS FOR GROUP PROJECT

Your group has been discussing a holistic view of the gospel message and how we can live it out in tangible ways. Now you have an opportunity to take what you are learning and do something together. Be sure to plan this group project early and undertake it before your final group gathering. Following are three options you might consider.

Option One: Helping Widows

The apostle James says, "Religion that God our Father accepts as pure and faultless is this: to look after orphans and widows in their distress and to keep oneself from being polluted by the world" (James 1:27). There are widows in every neighborhood, many who are elderly and find it difficult to keep up with basic household tasks: cleaning the house, changing lightbulbs, raking leaves, cleaning gutters, shoveling snow, getting the oil changed in their cars, etc. Live out the gospel message by identifying widows in your faith community or neighborhood and offering to help them with whatever they need one Saturday morning. See your service as a tangible way to share God's love with those who are often neglected.

Option Two: Mentoring and Tutoring
According to a U.S. Census Bureau report, over 25 million children live apart from their biological fathers—that is 1 out of every 3 (34.5 percent) children in America (65 percent African-American children, 36 percent Hispanic children, and 27 percent white children). The need for mentors to invest in these children's lives is critical; it is a challenge to the American church to live the gospel by loving these children. Individually, or as a group, commit to volunteer with a local program such as Big Brothers Big Sisters of America (www.bbbs.org) that will match you with a child in a parent-absent situation. See more on mentoring through Donald Miller's Mentoring Project: www.thementoringproject.org. Or for a more introductory way to begin working with young people, contact the principal from your local school to offer semester-long tutoring help to students with academic needs.

Option Three: Visit a Prison
The prison system is one of those places where the human need for purpose, redemption, and restoration from brokenness is most obvious. Plan a time where your group can visit a local prison to help with a Bible study, training seminar, or mentoring program. Investigate whether any churches or organizations in your area already have programs that your group can participate in. Or, contact Prison Fellowship (www.prisonfellowship.org) or the International Network of Prison Ministries (www.prisonministry.net).

Preach the gospel at all times, and when necessary, use words.

FRANCIS OF ASSISI

I don't preach a social gospel; I preach the gospel, period. The gospel of our Lord Jesus Christ is concerned for the whole person. When people were hungry, Jesus didn't say, "Now is that political or social?" He said, "I feed you." Because the good news to a hungry person is bread.

DESMOND TUTU

If you believe what you like in the Gospels, and reject what you don't like, it is not the gospel you believe, but yourself.

AUGUSTINE

GROUP GATHERING FIVE

WHATEVER YOU DO FOR THE LEAST

EVALUATING THE PROJECT

DISCUSS

Over the past several weeks, you've been exposed to some new ideas. Your group has discussed and debated how these concepts might change the way you think about faith and culture. And you've worked on a group project together to begin considering how these ideas might change the way you live your lives. Spend some time evaluating what you learned during your group project.

DISCUSSION STARTERS

How difficult was it to undertake (or begin) your group project?

Did you find any part of it uncomfortable or not helpful? Why?

What's the most important thing you learned (or are learning) during your group project?

How are you able to see your project as a way of living out the gospel?

the whole gospel 101

THOUGHTS

SHEEP AND GOATS

REFLECT

Have a few people in the group take turns reading this section aloud.

Then journal your thoughts on page 105.

One day, just before he was crucified, Jesus talked with his followers about what would happen when he would reveal his glory, sit on his throne as King, and judge the people of all nations. Of course, he was speaking about his return, but the disciples didn't understand that he would be going anywhere, let alone be crucified.

Jesus used a common analogy, like he often did, by describing his role like that of a shepherd separating sheep from goats—true followers of his from those who weren't. The story still seems shocking:

> When the Son of Man comes in his glory, and all the angels with him, he will sit on his glorious throne. All the nations will be gathered before him, and he will separate the people one from another as a shepherd separates the sheep from the goats. He will put the sheep on his right and the goats on his left.
>
> Then the King will say to those on his right, "Come, you who are blessed by my Father; take your inheritance, the kingdom prepared for you since the creation of the world. For I was hungry and you gave me something to eat, I was thirsty and you gave me something to drink, I was a stranger and you invited me in, I needed clothes and you clothed me, I was sick and you

looked after me, I was in prison and you came to visit me."

Then the righteous will answer him, "Lord, when did we see you hungry and feed you, or thirsty and give you something to drink? When did we see you a stranger and invite you in, or needing clothes and clothe you? When did we see you sick or in prison and go to visit you?"

The King will reply, "Truly I tell you, whatever you did for one of the least of these brothers and sisters of mine, you did for me."

Then he will say to those on his left, "Depart from me, you who are cursed, into the eternal fire prepared for the devil and his angels. For I was hungry and you gave me nothing to eat, I was thirsty and you gave me nothing to drink, I was a stranger and you did not invite me in, I needed clothes and you did not clothe me, I was sick and in prison and you did not look after me."

They also will answer, "Lord, when did we see you hungry or thirsty or a stranger or needing clothes or sick or in prison, and did not help you?"

He will reply, "Truly I tell you, whatever you did not do for one of the least of these, you did not do for me."

Then they will go away to eternal punishment, but the righteous to eternal life.
– Matthew 25:31–46

Jesus is not suggesting that good works earn a righteous status with God. He and other biblical writers are clear that God's grace and salvation are entirely free gifts, given by God to undeserving sinners. This is the gospel. Nevertheless, those who hear this gospel message, respond to it, and follow Jesus, will live it out by showing that same grace and love to those in need.

Richard Stearns, president of World Vision, paraphrases a portion of Jesus' story for us today:

> For I was hungry, while you had all you needed. I was thirsty, but you drank bottled water. I was a stranger, and you wanted me deported. I needed clothes, but you needed more clothes. I was sick, and you pointed out the behaviors that led to my sickness. I was in prison, and you said I was getting what I deserved. (*The Hole in Our Gospel*, Thomas Nelson, 2009, p. 59)

REFLECTION STARTERS

Spend a few minutes journaling your thoughts to these questions, then share with the group.

How does this passage challenge or convict you?

What tangible needs exist in your community that you, your family, your Society Room group, or your church can address?

JOURNAL

the whole gospel   **105**

THE WHOLE MESSAGE

CONCLUDE

How do you view the gospel message differently as a result of this Q Society Room study?

What will change about your lifestyle in the future?

What will you start doing?

What will you stop doing?

Spend the last fifteen minutes of your gathering praying as a group. If you've never prayed in a group, don't let this intimidate you. Your prayers need not be elaborate or articulate. Simply talk to God. Use these suggestions to guide your time:

- Thank God for his saving grace when he:

    Created you and gave you purpose and meaning in life (your creation story).

    Rescued you from slavery to sin (your exodus story).

Restored you to wholeness and reconciliation with him (your exile story).

Made you clean and forgave your sin through Christ (your priestly story).

- Ask God for wisdom to see every aspect of your life (family, work, finances, hobbies, etc.) as an opportunity to embrace a holistic gospel.
- Ask God for creativity to live out the gospel message within your cultural channels of influence.
- Ask God for courage to live sacrificial lives of unconditional love toward others, especially those who are poor and marginalized.

Live the gospel.

Share Your Thoughts

With the Author: Your comments will be forwarded to the author when you send them to *zauthor@zondervan.com*.

With Zondervan: Submit your review of this book by writing to *zreview@zondervan.com*.

Free Online Resources at
www.zondervan.com

Zondervan AuthorTracker: Be notified whenever your favorite authors publish new books, go on tour, or post an update about what's happening in their lives at www.zondervan.com/authortracker.

Daily Bible Verses and Devotions: Enrich your life with daily Bible verses or devotions that help you start every morning focused on God. Visit www.zondervan.com/newsletters.

Free Email Publications: Sign up for newsletters on Christian living, academic resources, church ministry, fiction, children's resources, and more. Visit www.zondervan.com/newsletters.

Zondervan Bible Search: Find and compare Bible passages in a variety of translations at www.zondervanbiblesearch.com.

Other Benefits: Register yourself to receive online benefits like coupons and special offers, or to participate in research.